Original title:
When Emotions Sing

Author: Giselle Montgomery
ISBN HARDBACK: 978-9916-88-994-7
ISBN PAPERBACK: 978-9916-88-995-4

Memories in Melody

In the hush of twilight's glow,
Soft whispers of the past do flow.
Melodies linger, sweet and clear,
They dance like echoes, drawing near.

Notes entwine with dreams so bright,
Painting memories in the night.
Each chord a tale, each verse a song,
In this symphony, we all belong.

Time slips gently through my hands,
In rhythms made by distant bands.
The heart remembers every line,
In melodies, our souls entwine.

With every beat, a moment saved,
In harmony, the lost are braved.
Memories hum, in tune with grace,
A timeless dance we all embrace.

Embrace of the Ether

In the stillness of the night,
Stars whisper secrets, soft and bright.
The ether holds a gentle breath,
Cradling hopes, igniting rest.

Winds of change through branches weave,
A chorus of what we believe.
In shadows deep, the light may play,
Guiding us along the way.

Thoughts like mist, they swirl and blend,
In this space where dreams transcend.
Embracing all that we hold dear,
With every pulse, the world is near.

Moments float like drops of rain,
Filling hearts with joy and pain.
Together in this vast expanse,
We find a rhythm, we find our dance.

Anthems of Anguish

In shadows deep, our sorrows wake,
A haunting cry, a heart that breaks.
The echoes tremble through the night,
As hope retreats, out of our sight.

With every tear, a story bled,
In silent rooms where dreams have fled.
We wear our pain like a worn-out cloak,
In whispered tales, our spirits choke.

Crescendo of Compassion

A tender hand to heal the heart,
In solace found, we play our part.
The warmth of love, a guiding light,
Together strong, we face the fight.

In gentle words, our spirits soar,
With every act, we give, restore.
A chorus sings of empathy,
In harmony, we set hearts free.

Notes of Nostalgia

In fading light, the memories glow,
A whisper soft where soft winds blow.
Time's echo rings in the heart's refrain,
Each note a balm for love and pain.

The past unfolds in shades of gold,
In fleeting moments, stories told.
With every glance, a cherished face,
In heartstrings tied, we find our place.

Symphony of Solitude

In stillness deep, where shadows creep,
A lone refrain begins to weep.
Each breath a note, a silent song,
In quietude, where souls belong.

The heart, a drum, in rhythm beats,
In phases soft, a symphony meets.
With echoes of the self embraced,
In solitude, we find our space.

Ballad of Forgotten Dreams

In shadows cast by fleeting light,
Whispers of the past take flight.
Echoes of a child's sweet song,
Now fade gently, all too long.

Once a spark inside the heart,
Now a canvas torn apart.
Memories that softly gleam,
Drift away like distant dream.

Crescendo of Longing

Underneath the silver moon,
Hearts beat in a silent tune.
Waves crash softly on the shore,
Yearning for what was before.

Every sigh a whispered plea,
For the love that used to be.
In the night, the echoes swell,
Filling dreams with tales to tell.

Serenade of Silent Tears

Beneath a veil of midnight's grace,
Lonely souls find their place.
Each tear falls like softest rain,
Carving paths through hidden pain.

A serenade without a sound,
In the stillness, love is found.
Hearts entwined in shadows deep,
In silence, secrets quietly weep.

Harmonies of the Unseen

In the air, a melody sways,
Invisible through light of days.
Songs of moments yet to come,
Harmonies where dreams are strum.

Voices echo in the void,
Threads of fate they softly buoyed.
A symphony that knows no end,
In the heart, where hopes ascend.

Dances of the Unexpressed

In shadows where silence lies,
Whispers weave through tangled sighs.
A heartbeat drifts, a secret's grace,
In movements lost, we find our place.

With every glance, a story told,
In quiet glimmers, dreams unfold.
The language forged in silent breath,
A dance of life that conquers death.

A Tapestry of Tears

Threads of sorrow gently spun,
Moments captured, each undone.
In patterns rich, emotions flow,
A tapestry of pain and glow.

Through woven hearts, our stories cry,
In the depths, where shadows lie.
Yet from the tears, we stitch a smile,
Creating beauty all the while.

Chiming of Elysium

Bells of joy in radiant chime,
Heralding love through space and time.
In melodies of a peaceful song,
Where spirits gather, we belong.

The echoes dance on gentle air,
In every note, a whispered prayer.
Elysium calls with open arms,
Awakening hearts to nature's charms.

The Aria of Unfettered Hearts

In the night, our voices rise,
An aria spoken 'neath the skies.
Unfettered dreams in harmony,
We sing of love, wild and free.

With every note, we break the chains,
In freedom found, our spirit reigns.
Together in this vast expanse,
We find our truth in endless dance.

Chords of Connection

In the silence, a whisper sings,
Fingers brushing, electric strings.
Hearts in rhythm, softly align,
Melodies weaving, yours and mine.

Under starlight, the music flows,
Ebbing gently where love bestows.
Harmony blooms in shared embrace,
Defining moments, love's true grace.

Canvases of Emotion

Brushes dance on the canvas bright,
Colors blending, day turns to night.
Each stroke tells of joy and despair,
A tapestry woven with tender care.

Shadows linger where feelings dwell,
In every hue, a tale to tell.
Artistry blossoms, hearts laid bare,
Capturing dreams in the open air.

The Heart's Hidden Orchestra

Strings are strummed in twilight's glow,
A symphony only lovers know.
Rhythms pulse beneath the skin,
In silence, we hear the music begin.

Conducting emotions that rise and fall,
The heart's quiet song, the sweetest call.
In unseen harmonies, we find our way,
A timeless dance, night and day.

Unspoken Synchrony

Eyes lock, a moment holds the space,
Words unneeded, we share the grace.
Heartbeat echoes in the quiet room,
A language crafted beyond the gloom.

Two souls merging in perfect time,
Silent vows spun like a rhyme.
In the pauses, our connection grows,
A symphony only our spirit knows.

Fragments of Flight

In a sky of broken dreams,
Wings that once held grace,
Drift on whispers of the past,
Silent echoes leave no trace.

Clouds of doubt weave tightly,
Shadows dance with flickering light,
Each feather tells a story,
Of struggles lost from sight.

Scattered hearts in twilight,
Searching for a patch of blue,
Yet the wind carries softly,
Hope in each breath anew.

The Resonance of Reminiscence

Faded photographs in hand,
A time when laughter bloomed,
Memories linger like whispers,
In corners where shadows loom.

Each smile captured forever,
A tale of fleeting grace,
Yet the heart carries the journey,
In every worn-out place.

Time's river flows unceasing,
Yet we chase its fleeting glow,
In the silence of remembrance,
Love continues to grow.

Melodic Mosaics

Colors blend in harmony,
Notes that intertwine and sway,
Each sound a unique story,
Carved in the light of day.

Rhythms pulse like gentle waves,
Beneath the sun's warm embrace,
Creating art in motion,
In life's unending race.

In the heart's quiet corner,
Echoes of laughter resound,
With each step, a symphony,
In the beauty we have found.

Voices of Vulnerability

Whispers in the shadows speak,
Hearts exposed, a fragile thread,
In the silence, truths awaken,
Words unsaid leave us misled.

Courage blooms in open hearts,
A tapestry of scars we weave,
Through the cracks, our spirit shows,
In each wound, a tale to believe.

Sharing dreams beneath the stars,
Together we rise, unbroken,
In the warmth of shared stories,
Lives entwined, our voices spoken.

Tides of Tempest

Waves crash with a roaring might,
The sky darkens, eclipsing light.
Whispers claim the raging sea,
Nature's dance, wild and free.

Lightning strikes with fierce intent,
The ocean's spirit, heaven-sent.
In the storm, a tale unfolds,
Of sailors brave and hearts of gold.

Echoes in the Abyss

Deep below, where shadows dwell,
An ancient whisper casts its spell.
Secrets float on currents strong,
In the depths, where dreams belong.

Voices call from far away,
Fading tunes of yesterday.
In the silence, truths collide,
In the abyss, shadows hide.

The Sound of Sparks

Fireflies blink in twilight haze,
Like dreams igniting, setting ablaze.
With each crackle, a story starts,
Whispers of echoes, beating hearts.

Fleeting moments, a dazzling show,
Dancing bright in the night's glow.
Each spark holds a wish untold,
Glittering treasures, daring and bold.

Journeys in Rhythm

Footsteps echo on cobblestone,
Each path leads to the unknown.
Beats of life, a constant sway,
Moving us in a rhythmic play.

With every turn, a tale unfolds,
Of wanderers and secrets old.
Songs of love and paths once trod,
In journeys grand, we find our God.

Rhythms of Joy and Sorrow

In laughter's light, we dance and sway,
Yet shadows linger, dark and gray.
The heart beats soft, then pounds with grace,
In every joy, a hidden trace.

The sun will rise, then fade away,
With every night, we find our way.
A fragile line, we walk anew,
In joy and sorrow, life's debut.

Through valleys deep, we learn to climb,
In silent tears, we find our rhyme.
Embrace the light, accept the dark,
For truth resides within each spark.

A bittersweet, harmonious song,
In rhythms deep, where we belong.
For joy and sorrow's woven thread,
In the fabric of our lives, we're led.

The Song of Hidden Feelings

In quiet rooms, emotions swell,
Behind closed doors, we weave our spell.
A smile disguises tears unspilled,
In silent worlds, our hearts are filled.

The whispers echo, soft and faint,
As hidden colors blur the paint.
We sing of dreams, yet never share,
In unspoken words, we're laid bare.

Each glance a story, left untold,
In secrets kept, our hearts grow bold.
Together apart, we dance alone,
In harmony, yet never known.

For every longing, every ache,
A melody that we must break.
The song within, we yearn to find,
In hidden feelings, hearts aligned.

Cadence of the Mind

Thoughts are whispers in the night,
Echoes dance in fleeting light.
A rhythm flows through every crack,
In scattered dreams that call us back.

In silent chambers, visions blend,
And wandering paths will twist and bend.
Beyond the chaos, purpose lies,
In simple truths and endless skies.

The pulse of time, a steady beat,
In every heart, the world's deceit.
As moments clash, we seek to find,
The gentle peace within the mind.

In thoughtful pause, we learn to see,
The symphony of what could be.
With every breath, we start anew,
In cadence sweet, we will pursue.

Sonnet of the Unspoken

In silent rooms where shadows play,
Words unvoiced weave dreams astray.
The echoes linger, soft, serene,
In corners where we've seldom been.

A whispered thought, a fleeting glance,
In uncharted realms, we dare to dance.
With every sigh, our stories flow,
In the unspoken, love will grow.

A tapestry of hopes concealed,
In every heart, the truth revealed.
The warmth of closeness, yet apart,
In silent bonds, we share our heart.

For in the hush where words rescind,
The deepest ties will find their wind.
In sonnets soft, we speak our truth,
In unspoken love, we find our youth.

Unraveled in Rhyme

Threads of thought dance in the air,
Tangled dreams beyond compare.
Words like jewels, they softly gleam,
Unraveled tales, a whispered dream.

In shadows deep, the stories hide,
Where echoes linger, and hopes abide.
With every note, a truth unwinds,
In rhythmic flows, our fate defines.

Through laughter's grace and sorrow's sting,
The notes they rise, the heart takes wing.
Weaving phrases, a tapestry bright,
Unraveled in the soft moonlight.

Cadence of the Unseen

In twilight's hush, the world awakes,
With every heartbeat, the silence quakes.
Invisible threads connect us all,
In cadence soft, we rise or fall.

Stars whisper secrets in the night,
Guiding lost souls with their light.
Each moment drips with delicate grace,
Unseen rhythms, a timeless embrace.

The pulse of life beneath our skin,
A dance of shadows, where dreams begin.
In silence heard, the truth reflects,
A symphony of life that connects.

Serenading the Stars

Under the cloak of a velvet sky,
Lullabies echo where memories lie.
Faint glimmers flicker, stories unfold,
Serenading the stars, both timid and bold.

With every heartbeat, the universe sighs,
A cosmic chorus, where wonder lies.
Their shimmering paths are whispers of fate,
Guiding our journey, it’s never too late.

Each twinkling light, a dream set free,
Calling the wanderers home to see.
In the stillness, the night does sing,
Serenading the stars, a celestial ring.

Whispers in the Wind

Breezes carry tales from afar,
Softly spoken, like a distant star.
Nature’s sigh, a gentle embrace,
Whispers in the wind, time leaves no trace.

Through rustling leaves, the secrets flow,
Echoing truths we long to know.
With every gust, a story spins,
In the heart’s quiet, the journey begins.

Windswept dreams drift through the trees,
A melody hums, floating with ease.
In every breath, a mystery finds,
Whispers in the wind, soft, unconfined.

Echoes of Euphoria

In the twilight's gentle embrace,
Whispers of joy find their place.
Dancing shadows, laughter bright,
Moments captured in the night.

Chasing stars with open hearts,
Dreams alight as daylight departs.
Echoes linger, a sweet refrain,
Binding souls like soft, warm rain.

The world spins in a vibrant hue,
Every moment feels brand new.
Fleeting glimpses, joy we find,
In the chaos, love's entwined.

With every breath, we rise and soar,
In the echoes, forevermore.
Together, we paint the skies,
With euphoria in our eyes.

Ballads of the Broken

In hollow halls where silence weeps,
The heartache deep, the memory keeps.
Whispers of love once bright and fair,
Now lost in shadows, heavy despair.

Fragments scattered, voices fade,
Promises made in the twilight's shade.
We sing of pain, a somber tune,
In the dark, beneath the moon.

Yet every tear waters the ground,
New life sprouts from what’s been drowned.
With every crack, the light breaks through,
A ballad sung for the brave and true.

So we'll gather the shards of the past,
In the music, our spirits cast.
Together we'll rise from the ashes,
Find the strength where the heart clashes.

Harmonies of Hope

In gardens where the flowers bloom,
Hope dances free, dispelling gloom.
With every note, the heart takes flight,
In harmonies, we find our light.

Gentle breezes carry our dreams,
Flowing softly like silver streams.
Together we stand, united and strong,
In the chorus, we all belong.

Through storms we've walked, hand in hand,
In the struggle, together we stand.
The music of life plays on and on,
In the dawn, we rise with the sun.

Let the melodies guide our way,
In the shadows, we find our sway.
With harmonies lifting spirits high,
We'll weave our dreams into the sky.

Serenade of Yearning

Underneath the starry veil,
Whispers float on a moonlit trail.
Hearts in sync like timeless chimes,
Dreaming deep in quiet rhymes.

Each note a sigh, a longing plea,
A serenade for you and me.
In the stillness, passion grows,
In the shadows, love still flows.

With every heartbeat, time stands still,
Filling spaces, a gentle thrill.
Yearning whispers, sweet and low,
Guiding us where the wild winds blow.

In the twilight, our souls shall meet,
In every echo, a heart's heartbeat.
Together we'll dance through night's refrain,
In love's serenade, we'll break the chain.

Symphony of Shadows

Whispers dance beneath the moon,
Silhouettes in a soft tune.
Echoes play in the night air,
Secrets linger, everywhere.

Each shadow tells a tale of old,
In twilight's arms, the night unfolds.
A symphony of dark and light,
Guiding dreams into the night.

The stars join in with twinkling notes,
As dusk unravels, softly floats.
A harmony crafted by time's hand,
In the silence, we understand.

Frets of Frustration

Fingers ache on the worn strings,
Every note just misses things.
The melody slips from my grasp,
In the silence, my heart will gasp.

Chords of doubt fill the empty air,
Frustration whispers, it's not fair.
Yet still I play, through trials deep,
Hoping one day, the tune will leap.

In the struggle, a fire burns,
Each failed note, another turn.
But music's hope will never fade,
For in each fret, a dream is laid.

Melodies of the Memorable

Songs of laughter fill the air,
Moments cherished, beyond compare.
Notes that sparkle like the stars,
Each memory, a timeless jar.

Whispers of love in a sweet refrain,
Each harmony, a soft, sweet pain.
The echoes linger, day by day,
In every heart, they find their way.

Melodies wrap us in their grace,
Every note, a warm embrace.
Together we sing, side by side,
In the music, love will abide.

Compositions of Connection

Two souls woven in a song,
In the chorus, they belong.
Harmony flows, a gentle stream,
Together they weave a shared dream.

Each note connects, like fingers clasped,
In the rhythm, a bond is grasped.
Melodies swirl in sweet delight,
A dance of hearts, both day and night.

With every word, a story shared,
In the silence, they have dared.
Compositions of love's embrace,
In the music, they find their place.

Chasing the Dawn

In the hush before the light,
Dreams blend with the night,
Colors awaken in the sky,
Whispers of a day gone by.

Footsteps trace the golden line,
Where shadows and sunlight intertwine,
Hope rises with each breath,
Dancing on the edge of death.

Time shifts in soft embrace,
As morning paints the space,
Chasing hues of softest grace,
In the dawn’s gentle chase.

Beats of Belonging

In the heart, a rhythmic song,
Together where we all belong,
Echoes of laughter fill the air,
Moments held with tender care.

Unity in every beat,
Walking paths where friendships meet,
Each heartbeat a thread of gold,
Woven stories to be told.

In the circle where we stand,
Holding tight, hand in hand,
Pulse of life in every sigh,
Beats of love that never die.

Refrains of Redemption

In the shadows, a melody calls,
Stirring hope where darkness falls,
Each note a step toward the light,
Refrains breaking through the night.

Whispers of grace in the breeze,
Softly urging us to believe,
With every stumble, there's a chance,
To rise up and join the dance.

Through the trials, hearts will mend,
Seeking solace, hand in hand,
With every song, a promise new,
Refrains of life, forever true.

Poetic Pulses of Passion

In the quiet, feelings bloom,
Words breathe life, dispel the gloom,
Ink spills tales of love and fire,
As hearts ignite with raw desire.

Rhythms flow like rivers wide,
Where secrets and bold truths collide,
Every stanza, a burst of light,
Illuminating the darkest night.

Pulses race in every line,
Creating worlds where souls entwine,
In the dance of verse and rhyme,
Passion lives beyond all time.

Songs of the Spirit

Whispers weave through the night,
Carried on the wings of dreams.
Echoes dance in the soft light,
Awakening ancient streams.

Voices call from afar,
Guiding hearts on their way.
Luminescent like a star,
In the depths where shadows play.

Each note a sacred spark,
Filling silence with its grace.
In the stillness, we embark,
Finding solace in its embrace.

Melodies of hope arise,
Wrapping souls in gentle arms.
In the music, freedom lies,
Wrapped in nature's quiet charms.

Timeless Tunes of Tenderness

In every glance, a song is found,
A symphony of tender gaze.
In quiet moments, love is bound,
In soft, sweet, endless ways.

With every touch, a note is played,
Resting softly on the heart.
In the silence, love displayed,
A timeless work of art.

Hands entwined like roots below,
Growing deeper with each breath.
In the dance, our spirits flow,
Recording life, defying death.

These tunes, a gentle breeze,
Whispering through fields of gold.
In the heart, they aim to please,
Tales of love forever told.

The Language of Longing

In shadows cast by fading light,
Longing stirs within the soul.
Words unspoken, lost to night,
Filling emptiness as a whole.

Whispers echo through the air,
Silent prayers wrapped in despair.
Every heartbeat, a silent plea,
As the world spins endlessly.

Eyes that meet yet cannot stay,
Chasing dreams that slip away.
In the distance, sighs resound,
In the hush, our hearts are found.

Pages filled with tales untold,
Of a love that haunts the night.
In this dance, our hearts unfold,
Seeking comfort, chasing light.

Heartstrings in Harmony

Strummed gently like a lonesome tune,
Heartstrings hum in soft delight.
In the stillness, love’s maroon,
Guiding souls to the night.

Each note a cherished memory,
Binding hearts in a warm embrace.
As we sway in unity,
Time melts in this sacred space.

Fingers glide on strings so fine,
Creating echoes of our past.
In this moment, hearts entwine,
Finding peace, forever cast.

Together we weave our fate,
In melodies both light and deep.
In this symphony, we relate,
Harmony we’ll always keep.

A Chorus of Resilience

In shadows deep, we find our light,
With scars adorned, we rise each night.
A heartbeat strong, a will to stand,
Through storms we march, a hopeful band.

The whispers of the past, they fade,
Yet in their wake, we're unafraid.
We sing our truth, we lift our voice,
In unity, we make our choice.

Each tear a seed of strength will grow,
From fractured dreams, we learn to sow.
A tapestry of love and fight,
Woven with threads of purest light.

Together we embrace our fate,
With every step, we navigate.
A chorus strong, we'll never cease,
For in this life, we find our peace.

Notes from the Depths

In silence where the shadows dwell,
A symphony begins to swell.
A gentle hum from depths unseen,
It carries sorrows, sweet and clean.

Each note a whisper, soft and low,
Reflecting dreams we long to show.
Through waves of thought, the echoes weave,
In tangled tales, we learn to grieve.

The depths reveal what's true and real,
In every chord, the heart can feel.
A melody of loss, of gain,
In every note, a thread of pain.

Yet from the dark, the light will shine,
A harmony through space and time.
We rise from ashes, clear the haze,
With music's guide, we find our ways.

The Overture of Yearning

An overture of hearts aflame,
An echo calling out your name.
In every pause, anticipation,
A dream unfolds in contemplation.

Across the skies, the wishes gleam,
In twilight's glow, we chase a dream.
With every breath, a wish takes flight,
In shadows cast by fading light.

The stars above, they nod in grace,
Reflecting hope in every space.
We reach for worlds that lie beyond,
In every glance, a hidden bond.

With hearts aligned, we softly sing,
Of all the joys tomorrow brings.
A symphony of life and love,
A calling from the skies above.

Chiming of Inner Voices

In stillness, hear the chime within,
A symphony where dreams begin.
Soft voices rise, they intertwine,
A quiet truth, a sacred sign.

Each echo tells a tale so deep,
Of whispered hopes and secrets keep.
As shadows dance, the light will play,
In harmony, we find our way.

The mind's embrace, a gentle call,
Through fractured thoughts, we break the wall.
With every note, a truth we find,
In unity, our souls aligned.

So listen close, to what's inside,
In every chime, let love abide.
Together we will rise and soar,
With inner voices, we explore.

Adagio for the Affected

In shadows deep, where sorrows dwell,
A quiet song, a muted bell.
Soft whispers echo through the night,
Embracing hearts with gentle light.

The world moves on, yet pain remains,
Like distant stars in silent chains.
Each tear a note in life's refrain,
A symphony of joy and pain.

In stillness found, we learn to cope,
Through every chord, we weave our hope.
In melodies both sweet and strong,
We find the strength to carry on.

As whispers fade, and time stands still,
Resilience blooms, a steadfast will.
Through every trial, we rise anew,
In adagio, we find what's true.

The Pulse of Pain

A throb within, a living ache,
The heartbeats sync, the world will quake.
In every moment, shadows creep,
A restless tide, a haunting sweep.

Yet in the depths, a spark ignites,
A flicker of hope in darkest nights.
Amidst the struggle, strength is found,
Resilience rises from the ground.

Through tangled paths, the spirit weaves,
In whispers soft, the heart believes.
The pulse of pain, a teacher wise,
From bitter tears, the courage flies.

For in the ache, there's life to claim,
A raging fire in a gentle flame.
The pulse goes on, relentless beat,
In every trial, we find our feet.

Harmonies of Healing

In tender notes, a balm is found,
Where silence dances, life unwound.
With every breath, a chance to mend,
A symphony where sorrows bend.

Through gentle hands and open hearts,
We weave the thread of hopeful arts.
In each embrace, the healing glows,
Transforming wounds as love bestows.

Harmony sings in whispered tones,
Restoring spirits, binding bones.
In every chord, a story told,
Of fragile strength and spirits bold.

As echoes fade, new rhythms start,
A melody that soothes the heart.
In harmonies of healing light,
We find our way from dark to bright.

Trills of Triumph

In every struggle, a tale of rise,
A melody that pierces skies.
With every trial, a note is sung,
A victory that keeps us young.

The trills echo, a joyful sound,
In every heart where hope is found.
Through thick and thin, through highs and lows,
Resilience blooms, the spirit knows.

Together we stand, unwavering, proud,
A tapestry of voices loud.
In cheerful strains, we celebrate,
The song of life, we cultivate.

For every challenge faced with grace,
A triumph earned, we embrace.
In trills of joy, we forever sing,
The anthem loud of everything.

Echoing in the Abyss

In the depths where shadows dwell,
Whispers float like distant bells.
Secrets linger in the night,
Echoes dance in fading light.

Voices thrumming through the dark,
Moments lost, a fading spark.
Silence weaves a heavy shroud,
In the void where dreams are loud.

Waves of time crash on the shore,
Calling out for something more.
In the abyss, we find our song,
Yearning for where we belong.

The Soundtrack of Solitude

In the quiet, notes arise,
Softly sung beneath the skies.
Each heartbeat, a gentle tune,
Underneath the watching moon.

Life's melodies, bittersweet,
Lost in rhythms, incomplete.
Solitude, a friend and guide,
In its arms, I learn to bide.

Strings of longing fill the air,
Harmony found in despair.
In silence, echoes start to weave,
The soundtrack of what we believe.

Verses of the Weeping Earth

Fields of green with tears do flow,
Nature's grief, a tale of woe.
Mountains echo silent cries,
Underneath the heavy skies.

Rivers run with sorrowed dreams,
Carrying forgotten themes.
Leaves that fall with whispered sighs,
Speak of time that slowly flies.

In the soil, the stories hide,
Of the pain that must abide.
Yet from ashes, life will rise,
Verses written in the skies.

The Symphony of Our Selves

Within us all, a symphony,
Notes that blend in harmony.
Voices join in vibrant dance,
Life composed by fate and chance.

Dreams and hopes, a chorus swell,
Every heartbeat casts a spell.
In the chaos, find your way,
Melodies of night and day.

Strings of joy and pain entwined,
In this music, truth defined.
We are notes in time's embrace,
The symphony of the human race.

Lament of the Lonely

In the silence of the night,
Echoes whisper my plight.
A shadow walks by my side,
In the darkness, there’s no guide.

Stars above seem so far,
Hiding dreams where they are.
Each tear, a memory fades,
In this silence, hope degrades.

Walls around me, cold and bare,
No one hears my silent prayer.
I reach out, but grasp the air,
Loneliness, my only care.

Yet still within, a flicker glows,
A spark where the heart knows.
A promise of dawn to chase,
In solitude, I find my place.

Songs from the Shadows

In the twilight, voices sigh,
Stories woven, spirits fly.
Hidden tales that haunt the deep,
In the shadows, secrets keep.

Melodies of joy and pain,
Drifting softly like the rain.
In the corners, laughter lingers,
Flickers dance on lonely fingers.

Echoes murmur, life uncertain,
Behind the veil, a glimmering curtain.
Winds convey a subtle tune,
Songs that rise beneath the moon.

In the hush, my heart will sing,
Embracing all that shadows bring.
Through the dark, a light may shine,
In the depths, a heart divine.

Rhythms of Regret

Time ticks softly, haunting rhymes,
Whispers lost in forgotten times.
Choices linger, shadows cast,
Moments cherished, fading fast.

Every heartbeat, echoes role,
Carved in memory, etched in soul.
A dance of choices, lives entwined,
In the corridors of the mind.

Fate’s cruel hand, the path not taken,
Silent walls where dreams lie shaken.
Regret comes like a gentle tide,
Flowing forth with nowhere to hide.

Yet from the sorrow, strength may grow,
In the depths, the heart can know.
Forging futures from the past,
In the rhythm, life held fast.

Rhapsody of Resilience

From the ashes, I will rise,
With a heart that won't disguise.
Every wound, a tale of strength,
Hope unfolds at great length.

Storms may rage, but so will I,
With each tear, I learn to fly.
In the struggle, I find grace,
In the shadows, I embrace.

Lines of courage, drawn in flight,
Crafting dreams in darkest night.
Through the fire, I will transcend,
In this journey, I will mend.

Rhapsody of life, I’ll sing,
With every challenge love will spring.
For in every fall, I will know,
The power in resilience grow.

Whispers of the Heart

In the silence, soft words dance,
A gentle breeze, a fleeting glance.
Secrets linger in the air,
Whispers soft, a lover's prayer.

Moonlight kisses on the skin,
Lost in dreams, where love begins.
In each heartbeat, stories told,
In quiet night, the warmth of gold.

Stars above, twinkling bright,
Guide the souls through the night.
With every sigh, a sweet refrain,
In the dark, love's tender gain.

Hold me close, don’t let go,
In this moment, time is slow.
Whispers woven with delight,
In the heart, love's pure light.

Symphony of Shadows

In twilight's arms, shadows play,
A melody of night and day.
Whispers echo through the trees,
Nature’s song on gentle breeze.

Silent notes of dusk arise,
Painting dreams across the skies.
Underneath the moon's soft gaze,
Light and dark in perfect phase.

Each heartbeat sings a hidden tune,
Under the watchful eye of the moon.
Harmony in the still night air,
Symphony in love's sweet care.

As the stars join the song,
Night reveals where we belong.
In the dance of shadow and light,
Life unfolds in sheer delight.

Echoes of Tenderness

Softly calls the evening breeze,
Whispers float among the trees.
In the stillness, hearts align,
Echoes deep, a love divine.

Every glance, a secret shared,
Through the silence, love declared.
Gentle smiles, tender grace,
In their eyes, a sacred space.

Moments linger, soft and sweet,
In each heartbeat, love's heartbeat.
Waves of warmth, a soothing balm,
In this quiet, find your calm.

Through the echoes, soft and light,
Love awakens in the night.
In the depth of every sigh,
Tenderness will never die.

Chords of the Soul

In the silence, strings do hum,
Soft vibrations, hearts become.
Melodies of dreams unfold,
In the warmth, a story told.

Each note dances like a flame,
Calling out, it speaks your name.
Harmony of heart and mind,
In this rhythm, love we find.

When the world is fast asleep,
In the shadows, secrets keep.
Chords entwined, a perfect blend,
In this music, hearts transcend.

Let the music sweep us high,
On the wings of a lullaby.
In the symphony of the night,
Chords will lead us to the light.

Surrender to the Symphony

Close your eyes, hear the sound,
Whispers of joy all around.
Strings and winds in harmony,
A world alive, wild and free.

Let the rhythm take your soul,
Feel the music make you whole.
Every note a gentle push,
In this moment, find your hush.

With each beat, let worries fade,
In the symphony, be remade.
Dance with shadows, chase the light,
In surrender, find the night.

The Pulse of Perception

Awake in hues of soft dawn,
Where reality unspawns.
Feel the pulse beneath your skin,
Echoes of the world within.

Every glance a story spun,
In the weave of everyone.
Listen closely to the air,
Secrets linger everywhere.

Time unfurls in quiet beats,
Witness where the heart repeats.
In the stillness, truths emerge,
A gentle wave, a mindful surge.

Songbirds of Solace

In the wood, where shadows twine,
Songbirds sing their sweet design.
Melodies that warm the heart,
From their tunes, we'll never part.

Dancing trees in softest breeze,
Whispers shared with tender ease.
Every chirp a soft embrace,
Time suspended in this space.

In their lullabies, we're found,
Floating high above the ground.
Nature's choir, ever near,
Through their song, we conquer fear.

The Rhyme of Revelry

In the night, where spirits blend,
Joyous laughter knows no end.
Raise your glass to moments bright,
In this dance of sheer delight.

Let the music swell and rise,
Beneath the stars, we realize.
Every heartbeat keeps the time,
Lost in love, we find our rhyme.

Celebrate the bonds we share,
In this chaos, life is rare.
With each step, we carve our name,
In the rhythm, we stake our claim.

Echoing Echoes of Love

In whispers soft, our hearts entwine,
Moments linger, like aged wine.
Through shadows cast, our feelings grow,
In every glance, our secrets flow.

Summer nights under fading stars,
We share our dreams, and heal our scars.
The world may spin, yet here we stand,
In echoes sweet, love's gentle hand.

With every pulse, the memory's sweet,
In rhythm's dance, our spirits meet.
Together bound, like waves in tide,
In echoes true, where hearts abide.

Forever held in heart's embrace,
In quiet moments, we find our place.
Echoing love, a timeless song,
In every breath, where we belong.

Serenades for the Soul

In twilight's glow, the soft notes rise,
A symphony beneath the skies.
With every chord, our minds align,
In harmony where hearts combine.

The gentle strum of strings will play,
Melodies that guide the way.
In whispered tones, our wishes soar,
The essence of what we adore.

From distant lands, the rhythms call,
A serenade that conquers all.
Through laughter's grace, and tears that fall,
In every sound, we stand enthralled.

Each note a breath, a story told,
In music’s warmth, we find the gold.
Together, we shall sing anew,
Serenades for hearts that grew.

The Sound of Silence

In quietude, the echoes play,
A haunting song that fades away.
In stillness wrapped, we search for light,
In silence found, the world feels right.

Between the thoughts, a gentle sway,
Where whispers dance and shadows stay.
The heartbeats soft, a tender sign,
In tranquil moments, our souls align.

Lost in the depths of muted sighs,
In every pause, the truth lies.
In silent strength, we find our might,
A bond unbroken, in the night.

Through quiet spells, we rise and stand,
In shadows cast, we hold each hand.
The sound of silence, pure and clear,
In every heartbeat, love draws near.

Crescendos of Clarity

With every rise, the spirit soars,
In crescendos bright, open doors.
Insight unfolds, a brilliant view,
In heart's embrace, we start anew.

From depths unknown, we climb the height,
In clarity’s glare, we find our light.
In every struggle, a lesson learned,
Through storms we weather, passions burned.

Voices strong, we lift our song,
In unity where we belong.
Through highs and lows, together stride,
In clarity's glow, we will abide.

So let the music play its role,
In crescendos deep, it heals the soul.
With hope in hand, we'll journey far,
In every note, our guiding star.

The Language of Sentiment

Words weave softly between us,
A dance of hearts unspun,
Every whisper holds a promise,
In silence, we are one.

Emotions paint the canvas bright,
Shadows flicker, fears take flight,
In the gentle sigh of dawn,
A new beginning drawn.

Tears may form like morning dew,
Yet love's warmth can see us through,
With every heartbeat, truth unfolds,
In stories yet untold.

So let us speak in tender tones,
And let our feelings find their homes,
In the language that we create,
Love's secret we translate.

Melodies Beneath the Surface

There's a song beneath the silence,
A hum that fills the air,
Each note a fleeting promise,
Whispers linger with great care.

Soft echoes touch the shadows,
Dancing on an unseen stream,
Where dreams and thoughts play freely,
In a world that's but a dream.

Underneath the quiet laughter,
Symphonies begin to swell,
Each heartbeat sings a tale,
Woven in a fleeting spell.

So listen for the music,
A harmony of grace,
In the stillness of the moment,
Find your own sacred space.

Vibrations of the Heartstrings

A touch can raise the heavens,
A glance can stir the soul,
In the chamber of our longing,
We find what makes us whole.

Each heartbeat resonates like thunder,
In rhythm with the night,
Entwined in soft vibrations,
We dance till morning light.

With every gentle heartbeat,
A story starts to sing,
In melodies of passion,
We discover everything.

So let us strum the heartstrings,
A symphony composed,
In the music of connection,
Love’s path forever glows.

Lament of the Lonely Night

The stars twinkle in longing,
Embers of fading dreams,
In shadows where I wander,
Nothing's ever as it seems.

Whispers chill the murky air,
Ghosts of memories remain,
In the quiet of the evening,
I search to ease the pain.

Loneliness wraps like a blanket,
A shroud of endless night,
Yet in the depth of sorrow,
I still seek the light.

So I'll weave my wishes softly,
While the moon holds vigil near,
In the lament of the lonely,
Hope's echo is sincere.

Fragments of Fury

In shadows deep, a fire burns,
Echoes of rage twist and churn.
Whispers clash in a stormy night,
Fragments of fury take to flight.

Silent screams, a haunting tune,
Beneath the watchful, silent moon.
Scattered thoughts in a wild chase,
Chaos reigns in this dark place.

Hearts collide, a mirror breaks,
Shattered dreams leave aching aches.
Fury dances in swirling light,
Fractured souls lost to the fight.

Yet amid the ashes, hope might gleam,
A spark ignites a daring dream.
From fragments torn, new paths are made,
In fury's wake, the world won't fade.

The Dance of Desire

In twilight's glow, shadows sway,
Desire whispers the night away.
Softly, hearts begin to race,
A sultry rhythm, a warm embrace.

Stars twinkle, casting their dreams,
In moonlit pools where passion beams.
Two bodies arch, then seamlessly twine,
In the dance of love, the chords align.

Each step taken, a tender fight,
Cloaked in longing, lost in delight.
Fingers trace like a gentle breeze,
In this dance, they find their peace.

But desire burns with a fierce flame,
A fleeting rush, never the same.
Still they twirl, in time's soft grasp,
In the dance of desire, forever clasp.

Ballads Born of Bitterness

In echoes dark, the past returns,
With every tale, the heart still burns.
Bitterness weaves through every line,
Melodies born from sorrow's vine.

A heart once bright, now cloaked in gray,
Songs of loss, in shadows lay.
Harmonies clash like thunder's roar,
Each note a wound, a closing door.

Yet through the pain, a power found,
In whispered words, the lost resound.
Ballads drift on the winds of fate,
Each sorrow sung, no room for hate.

For from bitterness, strength does rise,
In every tear, a truth that lies.
Ballads speak of wounds that mend,
Finding solace as we transcend.

Celestial Chords of Cheer

Under skies of vibrant hue,
Celestial chords bring joy anew.
Stars align with a playful gleam,
In every note, a radiant dream.

Laughter dances on the breeze,
As hearts awaken, finding ease.
With every strum, the world ignites,
Celebrating love on moonlit nights.

Hope emerges from shadows past,
In melodies that hold us fast.
With each refrain, the spirit soars,
Celestial sounds knock down the doors.

Together we rise, hand in hand,
Creating tales across the land.
Celestial chords weave bright and clear,
With every heartbeat, cheer draws near.

Journals in Verse

In pages worn, the ink does flow,
Stories whispered, secrets grow.
Each line a step, a path to tread,
Memories linger, the words unsaid.

With every turn, the past awakes,
In silent words, the journey makes.
Through joy, through pain, the ink reveals,
The heart's embrace, the truth it feels.

Ink and paper dance in time,
Captured moments, rhythm, rhyme.
Each verse a star, in darkness shines,
A map of dreams, where hope aligns.

Forever bound, these thoughts in flight,
Caught in the depths of day and night.
In journals kept, our lives converse,
In every heartbeat, a verse rehearsed.

Cadences of the Heart

A gentle thrum, the pulse is clear,
Each heartbeat sings, a song sincere.
Rhythms rise and softly fall,
In whispers shared, we find our call.

Echoes linger in quiet grace,
With every glance, a warm embrace.
Time slows down, the world fades near,
In cadences, our love draws near.

Softest breaths, the night ignites,
In stillness, every dream takes flight.
The heart's own tune, a silent plea,
In melodies, forever free.

Together, we compose our fate,
In every note, we find our state.
Between the beats, our souls align,
In cadences, forever shine.

Messages from the Moon

A silver glow upon the sea,
In lunar light, our spirits free.
Whispers float on midnight air,
Messages sent, a love laid bare.

Drawn by tides, the pull so strong,
The heart remembers where it belongs.
In shadows cast by gentle beams,
We chase the light within our dreams.

Each crescent phase, a story shared,
In darkness found, souls unpaired.
Reflections dance on water still,
The moon's embrace, our hearts do fill.

Across the night, a silver line,
Connecting worlds, our lives entwine.
Messages received, softly spoken,
In moonlit nights, our vows unbroken.

The Heart's Echo Chamber

Within this space, love resonates,
An echo chambers, where fate waits.
Each whisper held, a tender sound,
In beats and breaths, our lives are bound.

Voices mingle, the past they weave,
In every tale, we dare believe.
The chambers hum, in soft reply,
With every heartbeat, we touch the sky.

Through ups and downs, the echoes play,
In joy and sorrow, come what may.
A symphony of hearts combined,
In unity, our souls aligned.

Time may fade, but here we dwell,
In the echo chamber, love's sweet spell.
Forever cherished, forever true,
In every echo, I find you.

Soliloquy of Sorrow

In silence deep, I dwell alone,
Where shadows whisper, seeds are sown.
Each tear that falls, a story lost,
A heart bears pain, a heavy cost.

The moonlight gleams on vacant halls,
A ghostly waltz in twilight calls.
Memories linger, bittersweet,
In every echo, life’s deceit.

Yet hope persists in depths of night,
A flicker soft, a distant light.
Through sorrow's veil, I search for peace,
In dreams where burdens slowly cease.

With whispered words, I take my stand,
Embracing pain, I understand.
In sorrow's song, I find my way,
A melody that leads to day.

Notes from the Night

The stars compose a silent tune,
While shadows dance beneath the moon.
A serenade of whispered dreams,
Where nothing's ever as it seems.

The nightingale begins to sing,
Her voice a balm, a softer wing.
In twilight’s arms, we find our grace,
In every note, we find our place.

The darkness offers secrets rare,
In whispers shared, a tender care.
Each haunting chord, a story spun,
In every dusk, a day begun.

Let the night cradle our fears,
With starlit hopes and falling tears.
For in the calm, a world awaits,
In night’s embrace, we find our fates.

Lullabies of Liberation

In gentle breezes, freedom sings,
A song that soars on whispered wings.
Each note, a promise, softly calls,
To break the chains, to risk the falls.

With courage born from deep within,
We rise anew, we learn to swim.
In tides of change, we'll find our shore,
And dance to dreams we've longed for more.

A lullaby for hearts unbound,
Where hope and strength are truly found.
In every heartbeat, we ignite,
The flame of love, pure, burning bright.

Let chains be myths of yesteryears,
Together strong, we face our fears.
In unity, we claim our voice,
In lullabies, at last, rejoice.

A Chorus of Colors

In morning light, a canvas spills,
With hues of joy, on verdant hills.
The sun does paint with golden grace,
Each shade a smile, each light a face.

The flowers hum a vibrant tune,
In every petal, spring’s cocoon.
A symphony of life unfolds,
In colors bold, the heart beholds.

In twilight's glow, the world resides,
With crimson dreams and azure tides.
Each sunset calls, a soft goodbye,
Yet promises of stars up high.

Embrace the hues that life bestows,
In every moment, beauty grows.
A chorus sung by nature's hand,
In colors bright, together stand.

Rhapsody of Revelations

In twilight's glow, secrets unfold,
Each whisper dances, stories told.
Stars above sing in a serene bliss,
Echoes of dreams, in the night's sweet kiss.

A crescent moon guides the way,
While shadows of doubt quietly sway.
Hope ignites in the heart's vast space,
Illuminating paths we bravely face.

Time weaves threads of fate and chance,
In every heartbeat, a sacred dance.
With every breath, the truth revealed,
A tapestry of life, endlessly sealed.

Awakening visions, passion ignites,
In the symphony of long-held sights.
With every note, new worlds arise,
In this rhapsody where wisdom lies.

The Sound of Stillness

In silence deep, the world retreats,
A gentle hush, where time repeats.
Whispers of nature, soft and light,
Bathe the soul in purest delight.

The rustle of leaves, a quiet song,
In this stillness, we all belong.
Moments linger, free from strife,
In the essence of simply being alive.

Echoes of truth in the calm air,
Speak to the heart, if only we care.
Listening closely to the mind's tune,
Finding solace beneath the moon.

With every heartbeat, peace we gain,
In realms of stillness, we break the chain.
A sanctuary where thoughts can ease,
In the sound of stillness, we find our peace.

Whispers of the Heart

Softly the heart begins to speak,
In tender tones, it finds the weak.
With each pulse, a wish takes flight,
Painting dreams in the velvet night.

Gentle caress of hope and fear,
In every whisper, love draws near.
With open arms, we embrace the jest,
Finding strength in the silent quest.

The language of love, a sweet embrace,
Lingering warmth in time and space.
Through trials faced and laughter shared,
The heart's whispers, forever bared.

In longing gazes, we find our way,
Guided by love, come what may.
Each whisper a promise, a quiet start,
In the symphony of the beating heart.

Melodies of the Soul

In every heartbeat, music flows,
A dance of shadows, light bestows.
Harmony blossoms in quiet rooms,
As the spirit whispers, life resumes.

Strings of longing, plucked with grace,
In the cadence of a warm embrace.
Notes of laughter, echo so clear,
An orchestra of memories near.

The rhythm of dreams, a gentle sway,
Guiding the lost along the way.
In the silence, hear the song,
A melody where we all belong.

Let every note ring loud and free,
Carving paths of destiny.
As melodies intertwine and swell,
In the soul's music, all is well.

Cadence of Joy

In the morning light we dance,
With laughter sweet, a joyful chance.
The music swells, our spirits rise,
A melody beneath the skies.

In every stride, a soft embrace,
Happiness found in every place.
We sing of dreams, our hearts ignite,
Together we create the light.

Through fields of green, we wander free,
In every note, pure harmony.
With every step, our spirits soar,
In joy’s embrace, we’ll find much more.

So let us cherish every sound,
In the cadence of joy, we're found.
A symphony of life we weave,
In every beat, we shall believe.

Chords of Fear

In shadows deep, the whispers creep,
A haunting tune that stirs the sleep.
With quivering hearts, we face the night,
As chords of fear bring dimming light.

The echoes of what lies ahead,
Fill vacant spaces, wrap like thread.
Each note a tremor in the air,
An anthem born of silent prayer.

Yet through the dark, a spark may gleam,
A fragile thread that dares to dream.
In tension's grip, we learn to fight,
For hope can rise from depths of night.

So seize the fear, let courage swell,
In chords of fear, we'll weave our spell.
With every breath, we'll stand and face,
The haunting notes with strength and grace.

Verses of Vulnerability

In quiet moments, truth unwinds,
A tapestry of fragile minds.
With open hearts, we dare to share,
The verses born from depths of care.

In every line, a story spills,
Of hopes, of dreams, and muted thrills.
We bare our souls in whispered tones,
In vulnerability, we find our homes.

With tender words, we bridge the gap,
In honesty, our hearts unwrap.
A shared embrace, a gentle touch,
In verses soft, we learn so much.

So let's create a sacred space,
Where vulnerability finds its grace.
In every verse, our spirits soar,
In truth and trust, we're evermore.

Sonnet of Serenity

In quietude, the world slows down,
A gentle breeze, a soft renown.
The whispers of the trees confer,
Upon our hearts, a tranquil spur.

With every breath, the stillness grows,
In moments soft, our spirit knows.
The peace of earth, the sky’s embrace,
In serenity, we find our place.

As waves recede, the sands align,
A soothing balm, a sacred sign.
Within this calm, our souls take flight,
In melody of soft twilight.

So let us bask in nature's song,
In sonnet's peace, we all belong.
A harmony of life, so pure,
In serenity, our hearts endure.

Milton Keynes UK
Ingram Content Group UK Ltd.
UKHW022005131124
451149UK00013B/1013

9 789916 889954